DATE DUE

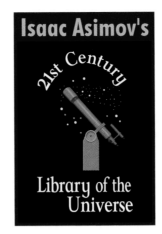

Isaac Asimov's

21st Century

Library of the Universe

Past and Present

Global Space Programs

BY ISAAC ASIMOV

WITH REVISIONS AND UPDATING BY RICHARD HANTULA

Gareth Stevens Publishing
A WORLD ALMANAC EDUCATION GROUP COMPANY

Please visit our web site at: www.garethstevens.com
For a free color catalog describing Gareth Stevens Publishing's list of high-quality
books and multimedia programs, call 1-800-542-2595 (USA) or 1-800-387-3178 (Canada).
Gareth Stevens Publishing's fax: (414) 332-3567.

Library of Congress Cataloging-in-Publication Data

Asimov, Isaac.
    Global space programs / by Isaac Asimov; with revisions and updating by Richard Hantula.
       p. cm. – (Isaac Asimov's 21st century library of the universe. Past and present)
    Includes bibliographical references and index.
    ISBN 0-8368-3982-X (lib. bdg.)
    1. Space sciences–Juvenile literature. 2. Astronautics–International cooperation–
Juvenile literature. 3. Outer space–Exploration–Juvenile literature. I. Hantula, Richard.
II. Title.
QB500.22.A82   2005
919.904–dc22   2005049027

This edition first published in 2006 by
Gareth Stevens Publishing
A Member of the WRC Media Family of Companies
330 West Olive Street, Suite 100
Milwaukee, WI 53212 USA

Series editor: Mark J. Sachner
Art direction: Tammy West
Cover design: Melissa Valuch
Layout adaptation: Melissa Valuch and Jenni Gaylord
Picture research: Matthew Groshek
Additional picture research: Diane Laska-Swanke
Production director: Jessica Morris
Production coordinator: Robert Kraus

The editors at Gareth Stevens Publishing have selected science author Richard Hantula to bring
this classic series of young people's information books up to date. Richard Hantula has written
and edited books and articles on science and technology for more than two decades. He was
the senior U.S. editor for the *Macmillan Encyclopedia of Science*.

In addition to Hantula's contribution to this most recent edition, the editors would like to
acknowledge the participation of two noted science authors, Greg Walz-Chojnacki and
Francis Reddy, as contributors to earlier editions of this work.

Printed in the United States of America

1 2 3 4 5 6 7 8 9 09 08 07 06 05

Contents

We live in an enormously large place — the Universe. It's only natural that we would want to understand this place, so scientists and engineers have developed instruments and spacecraft that have told us far more about the Universe than we could possibly imagine.

We have seen planets up close, and spacecraft have even landed on some. We have learned about quasars and pulsars, supernovas and colliding galaxies, and black holes and dark matter. We have gathered amazing data about how the Universe may have come into being and how it may end. Nothing could be more astonishing.

Human beings are at the beginning of an era of working and living in space. The United States, Russia, European nations, Japan, China, and other countries are involved in programs that will unite our planet in the vast endeavor of space exploration.

Space Age Rocketry

Rockets have existed in the form of fireworks for centuries. But Space Age rocketry began in 1903. That is when Russian schoolteacher Konstantin Tsiolkovsky developed the mathematics of rocket flight.

An American scientist, Robert H. Goddard, launched the first liquid-fueled rocket in 1926. In 1942, a German war scientist, Wernher von Braun, developed the first large rocket, the V-2. V-2s could travel for hundreds of miles before reaching their target. With this, Space Age rockets had arrived.

After World War II, the United States and the former Soviet Union began a race to see which would be the first to conquer space. The Soviets launched Earth's first artificial satellite, *Sputnik*, in 1957.

In 1961, Soviet cosmonaut Yuri Gagarin became the first man in space. Two years later, Soviet cosmonaut Valentina Tereshkova became the first woman in space.

Over the following several years, both the United States and the former Soviet Union sent probes to the Moon and the planets Venus and Mars. Finally, in 1969, U.S. astronaut Neil Armstrong became the first person to walk on the Moon.

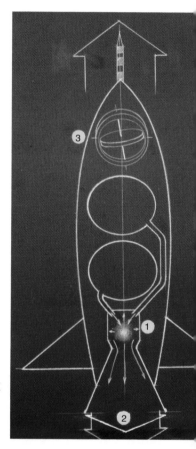

The rocket man

American rocket pioneer Robert H. Goddard spent years designing, building, and testing rockets. He even drew up plans for sending a rocket to the Moon. During World War II he tried to persuade the U.S. government to use his rockets as missiles.

When the war ended, U.S. officials studying the German V-2 rocket asked German scientists how they designed it. "We read all of Goddard's books," they said. But it was too late for Goddard to know — he died just five days before the war ended.

Below: In a liquid-fueled rocket, oxygen and fuel from storage tanks flow into the combustion chamber (*1*), burn, and create hot gases that race out of the engine through a nozzle (*2*). A guidance system (*3*) keeps the rocket on path. The hot gases escaping from the nozzle push on the rocket, sending it forward . . . just as the escaping gas of a balloon sends it forward (*4*).

The mighty *Saturn V* rocket, one of the most powerful ever built. It was used to take humans to the Moon in the U.S. Apollo program, and also to launch the U.S. *Skylab* space station in 1973.

5

Journey to the Moon

The U.S. Apollo program landed astronauts on the Moon six times between 1969 and 1972. Each mission put two astronauts on the Moon's surface.

The Apollo missions brought about 838 pounds (381 kilograms) of Moon rocks and soil back to Earth to be studied for clues about the Moon's early history. Unmanned spacecaft from the former Soviet Union also brought back some Moon material for study. Since the Moon is a world without wind, water, or erosion, the rocks on its surface have not changed for billions of years. From them, scientists are discovering more about what Earth was like ages ago.

The last Apollo Moon flight was in 1972. Since then, no one has set foot on the Moon. But the world did not abandon Moon exploration. Unmanned probes were sent to, or to the vicinity of, the Moon, by the United States, the former Soviet Union, Japan, and the European Space Agency.

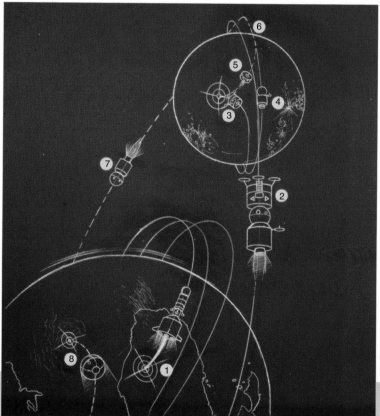

Above: A flight to the Moon — a rocket blasts off (*1*). The crew portion of the spacecraft joins its lunar lander craft after blasting out of Earth's orbit toward the Moon (*2*). After entering Moon orbit, the vehicles separate. The lander drops to the surface (*3*), while the other continues in orbit (*4*). After the lunar crew has explored the Moon, the lander blasts off (*5*), and the two crafts again join. The lunar lander is then discarded. The crew leaves lunar orbit (*7*). The crew capsule returns to Earth (*8*).

The European Space Agency's *Smart 1*
spacecraft began studying the Moon's surface
from lunar orbit in early 2005. The craft, using
an experimental solar-powered ion drive, took
a long time to reach the Moon. This diagram
shows the slow and winding path it traveled
after its September 2003 launch.

7

A Parade of Satellites

Thousands of artificial satellites have been launched into orbit around Earth. They come in all shapes and sizes. And they have many jobs to do.

Some study Earth itself – the health of forests and farms, or the location of fish and oil deposits. Weather satellites observe the atmosphere, photographing Earth's clouds and tracking dangerous storms. Navigational satellites guide ships, aircraft, and automobiles. Signals from navigational satellites are also used for such purposes as search and rescue operations, land surveying, and targeting of military weapons. Spy satellites eavesdrop on communications and use extremely sensitive cameras to watch for military movement. Space telescopes study the Universe from positions in the cosmos for a crystal clear view.

Besides Earth, spacecraft have also been put orbit around other bodies of the Solar System for exploration and scientific study. The Moon, the Sun, and some planets have received such artificial satellites.

Artificial satellites have been put into Earth orbit by the United States, Russia, China, India, and other nations, as well as by the European Space Agency and by Sea Launch, a group of four companies from the United States, Russia, Norway, and Ukraine that launches satellites from a platform in the Pacific Ocean.

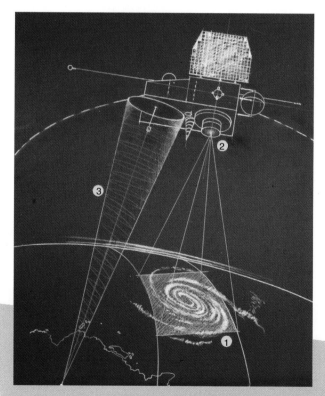

Above: The swirling clouds of a hurricane (*1*) are spotted by an orbiting weather satellite (*2*). The satellite tracks and studies the storm and beams pictures and data to scientists on Earth (*3*). This information gives scientists time to warn people threatened by such storms.

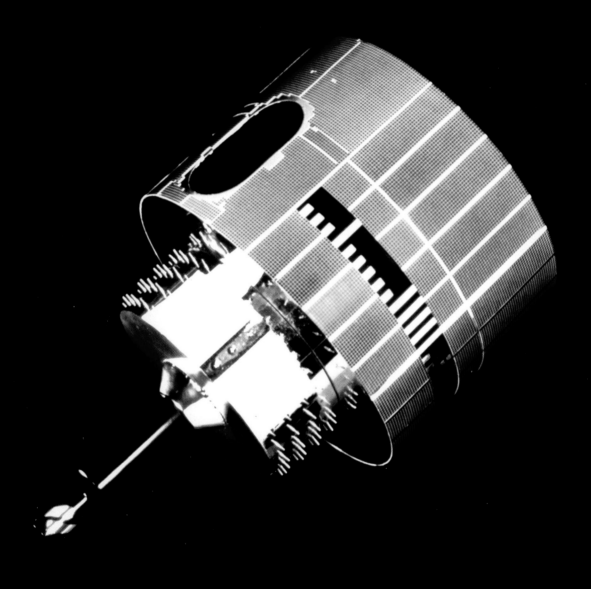

Europe's series of *Meteosat* weather satellites monitor weather patterns from 22,200 miles (35,800 km) up.

Above: A ground station linked to a communications satellite.

Right: Apollo 17 astronauts blast off from the Moon. But if they're in the spacecraft, who's taking this picture? The camera was controlled from Earth by radio signals. A transmitter on the Moon returned the signals in the same way.

Modern Communications

Without artificial satellites, our modern-day communications would be impossible. Because of satellites, today's radio, telephone, and television systems have a global reach. The Cable News Network (CNN), for example, can be seen in over two hundred countries and territories, thanks to the ability of communications satellites to relay signals across oceans and continents. This allows millions of people to see and hear events happening in every corner of the world.

In television and radio, communications satellites may be used to transmit programming from one ground station to another, or may be used to broadcast directly to receiving antennas on buildings and automobiles.

Countries that do not have the ability to launch their own communications satellites can buy launch services from other countries or from a multinational corporation such as Sea Launch.

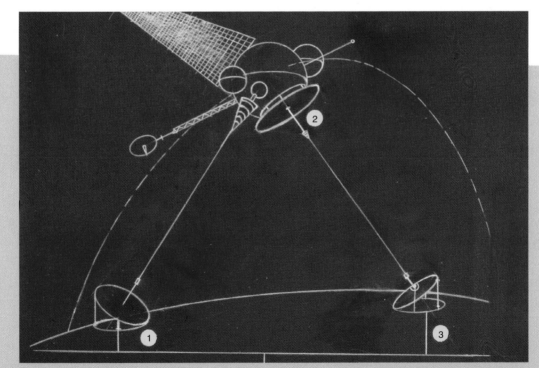

Above: A ground station on Earth (*1*) transmits TV or radio programs to an orbiting satellite (*2*). The satellite receives the signals and beams them to another ground station (*3*), which may be thousands of miles from the first.

Space Shuttles

The equipment used for launching humans into space is expensive. Because of this, space engineers worked for years to develop reusable spacecraft called space shuttles.

The first shuttle, *Columbia*, was launched in 1981 by the United States. Four more U.S. shuttles were later put into service. The shuttles did crucial work in space. They repaired damaged satellites in orbit, launched new satellites from space, and helped build the International Space Station. In addition, astronauts have carried out numerous experiments on board shuttles in the zero gravity of space. It was on the space shuttles that the first American women astronauts, Sally Ride and Judith Resnik, reached space.

The U.S. shuttle program, however, experienced serious accidents. The shuttle *Challenger* exploded during takeoff in January 1986, and *Columbia* was destroyed as it reentered the atmosphere in February 2003. In each disaster, all seven people aboard the craft were killed. NASA halted shuttle flights for a while after each disaster in order to make safety improvements.

A shuttle was built by the former Soviet Union, but it never came into use. Japan and the European Space Agency also have shuttle projects planned or in the works.

Opposite: In December 1993, shuttle astronauts took on a particularly challenging job — fixing the Hubble Space Telescope. They replaced the old solar panels and some other equipment and repaired a flaw in the telescope's main mirror.

Dangerous business . . .

Spaceflight is dangerous. Engineers try to make spacecraft and other equipment as safe as possible, but no one can foresee everything that might occur. Accidents can happen not only during a flight but also when astronauts are being trained and when equipment is being prepared for a flight.

The first person to be killed on a spaceflight was Soviet cosmonaut Vladimir Komarov, who died in 1967 when his craft crashed as it returned to Earth. The 2003 destruction of the space shuttle *Columbia* raised the total number of people known killed on spaceflights to at least eighteen.

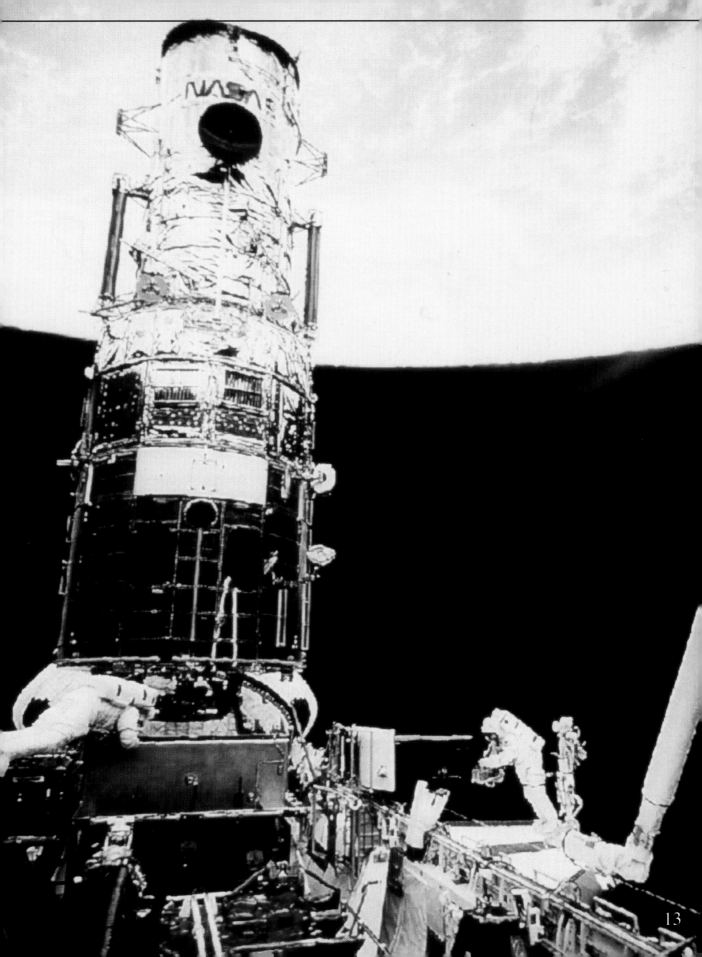

Above: SpaceShipOne, a reusable craft capable of rising just above the atmosphere and then landing. This simple spaceplane, launched from high in the air by a mother ship, made its first flights into space in 2004. It was the first privately developed craft to reach space.

Right: In the future, engineers may succeed in developing true spaceplanes that can take off and land like an airplane.

New Launch Vehicles

Although the U.S. space shuttle is basically reusable, its huge main fuel tank cannot be used again because it drops off and burns up in the atmosphere. In addition, the shuttle is a very complicated machine whose engines have to be rebuilt after each mission.

Engineers and designers believe that simpler launch systems can be created that would be partly or even completely reusable. In the United States a few private companies are working on inexpensive reusable vehicles for launching spacecraft into orbit. Researchers in several countries are also exploring the idea of SSTO or "Single-Stage-to-Orbit." Instead of using different rocket engines, or stages, that drop away during launch, an SSTO rocket would blast into orbit on one set of reusable engines. If it could be made light enough so as not to require too much fuel, such a design would probably be safer and less expensive to operate.

In time, true spaceplanes may be developed for travel to and from orbit. True spaceplanes would take off and land at runways, much as airplanes do today.

Meanwhile, nonreusable launch systems are still being studied by NASA and the aerospace industry. Such a system might be used with NASA's planned "crew exploration vehicle," which will someday carry astronauts up to the *International Space Station* and perhaps also to the Moon and Mars.

Left: Some ideas of what a "Single-Stage-to-Orbit" launch vehicle might look like.

A Cosmic Home

A space station is a satellite in orbit around Earth where people can live and do work, such as carrying out experiments and making scientific observations, for long periods of time. A few cosmonauts have spent more than a year on a space station before returning to Earth.

Several small space stations were placed in orbit near the end of the twentieth century, beginning with a series called *Salyut* that was launched by the former Soviet Union. *Salyut 1* orbited Earth for a few months in 1971. The last in the series, *Salyut 7*, was launched in 1982 and stayed in orbit for almost nine years. A somewhat larger U.S. station, known as *Skylab*, was launched in 1973 and remained in orbit until 1979. Still larger was *Mir*, placed in orbit by the former Soviet Union in 1986. It remained aloft for fifteen years.

The United States, Russia, Japan, the European Space Agency, and Canada are cooperating in the building of the even bigger *International Space Station*. Assembly in orbit began in 1998, and the first crew arrived in 2000.

Right: Cosmonaut Valeriy Polyakov, who boarded *Mir* on January 8, 1994, looks out *Mir*'s window during *Discovery*'s flyby.

Gravity — where would we be without it?

The Moon's gravitational pull is only one-sixth that of Earth's. Similarly, a space station in orbit around Earth could be made to spin to produce a gravity-like force, but it would be quite weak compared with Earth's gravity. What effect would a lifetime of weak gravity have on people? What would happen to babies born under such conditions? Would they ever be able to visit Earth with its higher gravity? Scientists don't know.

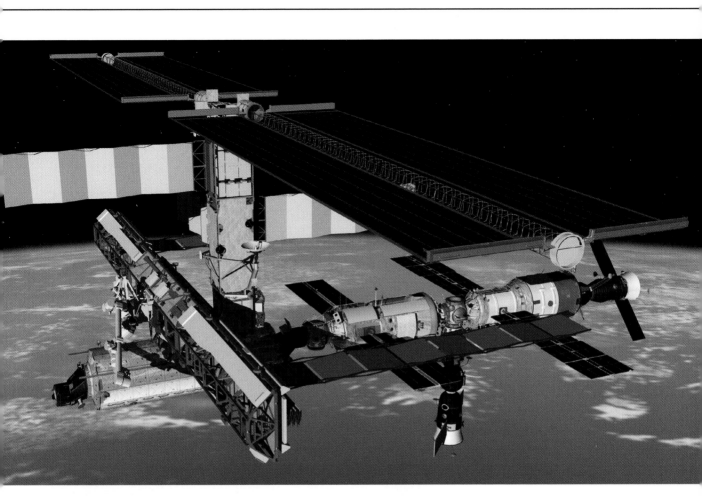

Above: An artist's view of the *International Space Station* in early 2004, when an unmanned Progress supply vehicle and a Soyuz spacecraft were docked at the station.

Right: In February 1995 the space shuttle *Discovery* inspected the Russian *Mir* space station in a close flyby. This set the stage for a docking of the two spacecraft later that year.

Into the Beyond

Someday, space stations could become Earth's launch pads for piloted flights to other planets. Because of the speed with which a space station travels in its orbit around Earth, a spaceship built there is already moving very fast. Launching it to the Moon and planets would be easier than a launch from Earth's surface because its engine would need less fuel. Also, a spaceship built in orbit won't be traveling through Earth's atmosphere, so bad weather would never delay a launch. And because there is no air resistance in space, a spaceship built in orbit will not need to have a pointed design.

A space station could provide a departure point for humans going to Mars and the asteroids. Space stations might also house huge settlements. Such a space station would be a self-contained world capable of holding thousands of people, who would make it their home.

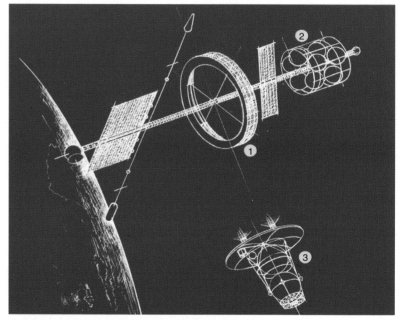

Above: An advanced space station might have a ring (*1*) that rotates to produce artificial gravity. To anyone in the ring, "down" would be toward the outside of the ring and "up" would be toward the central axle. Fuel and other supplies could be stored in another unit (*2*). Arriving spacecraft (*3*) could dock to take on supplies or unload cargo.

Air — a weighty subject!

In 1644, Evangelista Torricelli, an Italian scientist, proved that air has weight. His experiment helped scientists realize that air existed only near Earth's surface. Beyond Earth there was emptiness — a void. Torricelli, in a roundabout way, had discovered outer space. People traveling beyond Earth's atmosphere have to take their own air supply along.

Hollowing out an asteroid would create a strong shell for an artificial world.

Mapping New Worlds

The world's space programs are bringing us into ever closer touch with the rest of the Solar System. Before humans visited the Moon, probes had already mapped it in detail. Now the same pattern is holding true for Mars and the other planets. Unpiloted spacecraft – such as *Mariner*, *Venera*, *Pioneer*, *Voyager*, *Galileo*, and *Cassini* – have visited various planets and sent back data.

Spacecraft have mapped Mercury, Venus, and Mars. The four giant planets, Jupiter, Saturn, Uranus, and Neptune, and their satellites have also been studied. In 2005 a probe called *Huygens*, which had been carried by *Cassini*, penetrated the thick atmosphere of Saturn's huge moon Titan and gave scientists their first view ever of Titan's surface. The only planet that has not yet been studied by probes is Pluto.

Left: An artist's view of the spacecraft *Cassini* near Saturn's moon Titan. The small probe called *Huygens* has just separated from *Cassini*. *Huygens* landed on Titan in early 2005.

Cosmic rays – no laughing matter!

Cosmic rays bombard Earth from every direction. On Earth, the atmosphere protects us from most of the cosmic rays. In space, cosmic rays are more dangerous. If space settlements are built that can house thousands of people, how will they be protected from this radiation? On the Moon, perhaps settlements will be buried under the ground and shielded by a thick layer of lunar soil.

The European Space Agency's spacecraft *Mars Express* in orbit around Mars, as depicted by an artist. The craft reached the Red Planet in late 2003.

The Cosmos above the Clouds

Telescopes have long been one of the best ways to view the cosmos. But telescopes located on Earth all have the same problem — Earth's atmosphere. While the air surrounding our planet protects us from meteoroids and solar radiation, it can also distort our view of distant objects in space.

Telescopes outside the atmosphere are not affected by weather, temperature change, air pollution, or city lights. They can detect types of electromagnetic radiation that are unable to pierce Earth's atmosphere. They thus can potentially see farther, more clearly, and in greater detail than Earth-based scopes.

Telescopes located in space have detected black holes, distant galaxies, and incredibly powerful explosions, as well as evidence for the existence of planets orbiting many stars.

Space telescopes launched by NASA include a series of "Great Observatories" for different types of radiation. The series began with the Hubble Space Telescope in 1990, for visible, infrared, and ultraviolet light. It continued with the Compton Gamma Ray Observatory (in orbit from 1991 to 2000), the Chandra X-Ray Observatory (1999), and the Spitzer Space Telescope (2003), which detects infrared radiation.

Space observatories of various kinds have also been launched by such countries as Canada, Japan, and the former Soviet Union, as well as by the European Space Agency.

Left: The Chandra X-Ray Observatory, launched in 1999, orbiting high above Earth.

Opposite: An artist's rendering of the *Spitzer Space Telescope*, an artificial satellite that circles the Sun in an orbit trailing Earth.

The Moon: Earth's Sister World

Space exploration does not just mean going farther and farther into space. It also means exploring where humans have been before, and doing it more carefully and with greater cooperation among nations.

In 2004, U.S. President George W. Bush called for people to return to the Moon by 2020. Meanwhile, the United States, the European Space Agency, and such nations as China and Japan are working on new unmanned missions to the Moon.

Someday, humans will build mining stations on the Moon. From these stations, minerals will be obtained to build other structures in near-space. An observatory could be built on the far side of the Moon. Underground lunar cities may eventually house millions of people. The Moon will truly be a sister world of Earth.

Left: In this artist's conception of an astronaut exploring the Moon's surface, a reflection of the brightly lit lunar landscape gleams in the astronaut's visor.

Flights of fancy!

Writers have been imagining flights to the Moon since the time of the Roman Empire. They have told of adventurers being carried to the Moon by spirits, being blown there by waterspouts, flying there in chariots dragged by huge geese, or being drawn up by dew. In days gone by, Edgar Allan Poe wrote of space travel in a balloon, Jules Verne shot his explorers out of a giant cannon, and H. G. Wells imagined making use of an antigravity device.

An artist's conception of a small future supply base on the Moon.

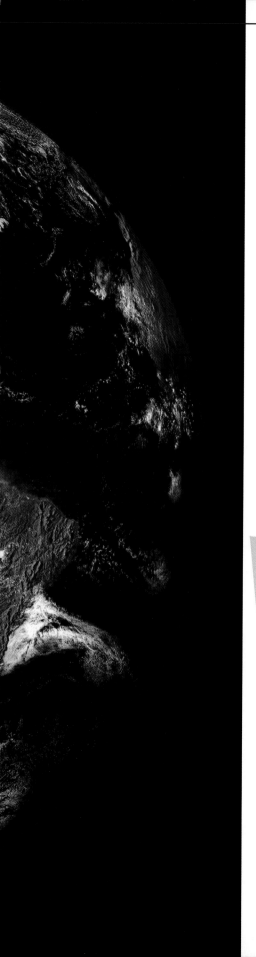

United in Space

One major aspect of global space exploration is that it is such a large and important project that individual nations cannot carry it through by themselves. The project provides an opportunity for many nations to work together, cooperatively, toward a common goal.

The vast distances of space make Earth seem small. Space contains huge amounts of materials, energy, and scientific data that the nations of Earth could cooperatively pursue. Because of space exploration, people may eventually come to identify themselves as fellow Earthlings, or, better yet, humans, and nothing else. Maybe, at last, people of all nations can learn to share this home of ours.

Left: A striking image of Earth and Moon, constructed from data provided by orbiting satellites. For vividness, mountains and valleys are shown as larger than they actually are.

Fact File: Stairway to Space

In the early years of the Space Age, in the 1950s and for most of the 1960s, space exploration was primarily a race — a "space race" — between the former Soviet Union and the United States. The Soviet Union took an early lead, launching the first artificial satellite, *Sputnik 1*, on October 4, 1957. The United States followed with its first satellite, *Explorer 1*, on January 31, 1958.

The sense of competition later faded. In 1967 the Outer Space Treaty, sponsored by the United Nations, went into effect. It states that the Moon and the rest of space are open to exploration by all nations and belong to none. Today, many nations cooperate on space projects.

A good example of nations working together is the European Space Agency, or ESA. Founded in 1975 by a group of European nations, with Canada later becoming an associate member, ESA pools the resources and knowledge of its member nations. Another example is the *International Space Station*.

Today, the major space-exploring nations launch satellites for countries that do not have their own rockets. The former Soviet Union and Russia (which took over much of the Soviet space program after the Soviet Union's 1991 collapse), as well as the United States, have played host to astronauts or cosmonauts from many different countries.

First Persons in Space, by Nation

SOVIET UNION (from 1992, RUSSIA)
April 12, 1961
Yuri Gagarin, aboard spacecraft *Vostok 1*, was the first person in space.

UNITED STATES
May 5, 1961
Alan Shepard, aboard spacecraft *Freedom 7*, was the first U.S. astronaut in space. On July 20, 1969, Neil Armstrong of *Apollo 11* was the first person to set foot on the Moon. On June 21, 2004, Mike Melvill, aboard *SpaceShipOne*, was the first person to fly a privately developed craft into space.

CZECHOSLOVAKIA
March 2, 1978
Vladimír Remek was a cosmonaut aboard Soviet space station *Salyut*.

BULGARIA
April 10, 1978
Georgi Ivanov was a cosmonaut aboard Soviet spacecraft *Soyuz*.

POLAND
June 27, 1978
Miroslaw Hermaszewski was a cosmonaut aboard Soviet space station *Salyut*.

GERMANY
August 26, 1978
Sigmund Jähn of East Germany was a cosmonaut aboard Soviet space station *Salyut*.

HUNGARY
May 26, 1980
Bertalan Farkas was a cosmonaut aboard Soviet space station *Salyut*.

VIETNAM
July 23, 1980
Pham Tuan was a cosmonaut aboard Soviet space station *Salyut*.

CUBA
September 18, 1980
Arnaldo Tamayo Méndez was a cosmonaut aboard Soviet space station *Salyut*.

MONGOLIA
March 22, 1981
Jugderdemidyin Gurragcha was a cosmonaut aboard Soviet space station *Salyut*.

ROMANIA
May 14, 1981
Dumitru Prunariu was a cosmonaut aboard Soviet space station *Salyut*.

FRANCE
June 24, 1982
Jean-Loup J. M. Chrétien, aboard Soviet space station *Salyut*, was the first French spationaut in space.

INDIA
April 3, 1984
Rakesh Sharma was a cosmonaut aboard Soviet space station *Salyut*.

AUSTRALIA
October 5, 1984
U.S. citizen Paul Desmond Scully-Power, aboard U.S. shuttle *Challenger*, was the first Australian-born astronaut in space.

CANADA
October 5, 1984
Marc Garneau was an astronaut aboard U.S. space shuttle *Challenger*.

SAUDI ARABIA
June 17, 1985
Sultan Abdul Aziz Al-Saud was an astronaut aboard U.S. space shuttle *Discovery*.

THE NETHERLANDS
October 30, 1985
Wubbo Ockels was an astronaut aboard U.S. space shuttle *Challenger*.

MEXICO
November 27, 1985
Rodolfo Neri Vela was an astronaut aboard U.S. space shuttle *Atlantis*.

SYRIA
July 22, 1987
Mohammed Faris was a cosmonaut aboard Soviet space station *Mir*.

AFGHANISTAN
August 29, 1988
Abdul Ahad Mohmand was a cosmonaut aboard Soviet space station *Mir*.

JAPAN
December 2, 1990
Tohiro Akiyama was a cosmonaut aboard Soviet space station *Mir*.

UNITED KINGDOM
May 18, 1991
Helen Patricia Sharman was a cosmonaut aboard Soviet space station *Mir*.

AUSTRIA
October 2, 1991
Franz Viehböck was a cosmonaut aboard Soviet space station *Mir*.

BELGIUM
March 24, 1992
Dirk D Frimout was an astronaut aboard U.S. shuttle *Atlantis*.

ITALY
July 31, 1992
Franco Malerba was an astronaut aboard U.S. space shuttle *Atlantis*.

SWITZERLAND
July 31, 1992
Claude Nicollier was an astronaut aboard U.S. space shuttle *Atlantis*.

KAZAKHSTAN
July 1, 1994
Talgat Musabayev was a cosmonaut aboard Russian space station *Mir*.

UKRAINE
November 19, 1997
Leonid Kadenyuk was an astronaut aboard U.S. space shuttle *Columbia*.

KYRGYZSTAN
January 22, 1998
Salizhan Shakirovich Sharipov was a cosmonaut aboard U.S. space shuttle *Endeavour*.

SPAIN
October 29, 1998
Pedro Duque was an astronaut aboard U.S. space shuttle *Discovery*.

SLOVAKIA
February 20, 1999
Ivan Bella was a cosmonaut aboard Russian space station *Mir*.

SOUTH AFRICA
April 25, 2002
Mark Shuttleworth was a space tourist aboard Russian spacecraft *Soyuz* and the *International Space Station*.

ISRAEL
January 16, 2003
Ilan Ramon was an astronaut aboard U.S. space shuttle *Columbia*. He was killed with other crew members when the *Columbia* was destroyed while reentering the atmosphere.

CHINA
October 15, 2003
Yang Liwei, aboard spacecraft *Shenzhou 5*, was the first astronaut of the Chinese People's Republic in space.

More Books about Global Space Programs

Artificial Satellites. Ray Spangenburg and Kit Moser (Franklin Watts)

Life Aboard the Space Station. Michael P. Belfiore (Lucent)

Man in Space: An Illustrated History from Sputnik to the Shuttle Columbia.
   Time Magazine (Time Inc. Home Entertainment)

Space. Andrew Chaikin (Carlton)

Space Exploration Reference Library. Rob Nagel and Peggy Saari (Thomson Gale)

The Space Shuttle: A Photographic History. Philip S. Harrington (Browntrout)

Space Stations. James Barter (Lucent)

DVDs

For All Mankind. (Criterion)

From the Earth to the Moon. (HBO)

Inside the Space Station. (Artisan)

Web Sites

The Internet is a good place to get more information about global space programs. The Internet sites listed here can help you learn about recent developments, as well as past history.

Encyclopedia Astronautica. www.astronautix.com
European Space Agency. www.esa.int/
NASA. www.nasa.gov/
Russian Space Web. www.russianspaceweb.com/
Spaceflight Now. spaceflightnow.com/
Windows to the Universe. http://www.windows.ucar.edu/

Places to Visit

Here are some museums and centers where you can find exhibits about global space programs.

Hong Kong Space Museum
Hong Kong Cultural Centre Complex
10 Salisbury Road
Hong Kong

H.R. MacMillan Space Centre
1100 Chestnut Street
Vancouver, British Columbia V6J 3J9
Canada

Kansas Cosmosphere and Space Center
1100 N. Plum
Hutchinson, Kansas 67501

National Air and Space Museum
Smithsonian Institution
6th and Independence Avenue SW
Washington, DC 20560

New Mexico Museum of Space History
Highway 2001
Alamogordo, New Mexico 88311

Space Center Houston
1601 NASA Road 1
Houston, Texas 77058

Glossary

Apollo: The U.S. space program that landed astronauts on the Moon several times between 1969 and 1972.

astronaut: a person who travels beyond the atmosphere of Earth. Russian astronauts are commonly known as cosmonauts, and French astronauts are called spationauts.

atmosphere: the gases that surround a planet, star, or moon.

black hole: a tightly packed object with such powerful gravity that not even light can escape from it.

cosmonauts: men and women from Russia or the former Soviet Union who travel beyond the atmosphere of Earth. Persons from other countries who fly on a space vehicle from Russia or the former Soviet Union are also sometimes called cosmonauts.

electromagnetic radiation: such forms of radiation as gamma rays, X rays, ultraviolet radiation, light, infrared radiation, radio waves, and microwaves.

erosion: the wearing away of an object or substance by such forces as wind, water, or ice.

European Space Agency (ESA): an organization founded in 1975 that pools the resources of several European countries and Canada for joint research and exploration of space.

galaxy: a large star system containing billions of stars. Our own galaxy is known as the Milky Way.

gravity: the force that causes objects like planets and their moons to be drawn to one another.

NASA: the space agency in the United States — the National Aeronautics and Space Administration.

navigational: having to do with planning or directing a craft's course or path.

observatory: a building or other structure designed for watching and recording celestial objects and events.

orbit: the path that one celestial object follows as it circles, or revolves around, another.

planet: a large celestial body that revolves around our Sun or some other star and that is not itself a star.

probe: a craft that travels in space, photographing and studying celestial bodies and in some cases even landing on them.

rocket: a vehicle used to launch satellites, probes, shuttles, and other craft into space. A rocket carries its own fuel and oxygen for burning, and it is driven forward by gases escaping from the rear.

rocketry: the study of, experimentation with, or use of rockets.

satellite: a smaller body that orbits a larger body. *Sputnik 1* and *2* were Earth's first artificial satellites. The Moon is Earth's natural satellite.

space shuttle: a mostly reusable space craft launched into space by a rocket but capable of returning to Earth under its own power. The first space shuttle, *Columbia*, was launched in 1981 by the United States.

space station: a large artificial satellite with enough room for people to live and work for long periods of time.

SSTO: Single-Stage-to-Orbit rocketry, the idea that instead of using different rocket engines, or stages, that are thrown away during launch, space explorers can use one set of reusable engines.

Index

Born in 1920, Isaac Asimov came to the United States as a young boy from his native Russia. As a young man, he was a student of biochemistry. In time, he became one of the most productive writers the world has ever known. His books cover a spectrum of topics, including science, history, language theory, fantasy, and science fiction. His brilliant imagination gained him the respect and admiration of adults and children alike. Sadly, Isaac Asimov died shortly after the publication of the first edition of *Isaac Asimov's Library of the Universe*.

The publishers wish to thank the following for permission to reproduce copyright material: front cover, 3, 5, 7 (large), 10 (lower), 13, 15, 16, 17 (both), 25, NASA; 4-5, 6, 8, 11, 14 (lower), 18, Matthew Groshek/© Gareth Stevens, Inc.; 7 (inset), ESA 2002, Illustration by Medialab; 9, Courtesy of Marconi Space Systems; 10 (upper), Courtesy of COMSAT; 14 (upper), Courtesy of Scaled Composites, LLC; 19, © Mark Maxwell 1989; 20, NASA/JPL; 21, ESA 2001, Illustration by Medialab; 22, NASA/CXC/SAO; 23, NASA/JPL-Caltech; 24, Mike Stovall and Mark Dowman/NASA; 26-27, NASA Goddard Space Flight Center.